The Heart of Meditation

Interflow

The Heart of Meditation

Interflow

George Breed

The Heart of Meditation: Interflow

Copyright © 2014 by Anamchara Books, a division of Harding House Publishing Service, Inc. All rights reserved. No part of this publication may be reproduced or transmitted in any form or by any means, electronic or mechanical, including photocopying, recording, taping, or any information storage and retrieval system, without permission from the publisher.

Anamchara Books
Vestal, NY 13850
www.anamcharabooks.com

IngramSpark Paperback ISBN: 978-1-62524-815-2
eBook ISBN: 978-1-62524-896-1

Author: George Breed
Interior design by Camden Flath.
Cover design by Ellyn Sanna.

Introduction

We have three minds: the animal mind, the logical-rational intellect, and a deep and open Awareness. In the pre-dawn morning, the three minds I am sit together quietly and expectantly for words to form, to arise from intuitive understanding. The brief sentences in this book are those words. They reflect a combination of animal consciousness, of rational intellect, and of something I like to call Merge. Blessings to you as your soul opens to these sentences. May we all continuously reclaim our Merge-inity!

1

Remember:
you are a phenomenon
embedded
in *the* Phenomenon.
More accurately,
you are
the Phenomenon
phenomening.

2

People say,
"However you define God."
But our Source
cannot be defined,
only experienced.

3

If you insist
on making a movie
of yourself,
remember:
you are the film—
and also the projector,
the screen,
the audience,
and the popcorn.

4

A true religion
is a vast ocean
with no bounds.
A belief system
is a circumscribed
floating dock
within that ocean.

5

You can't receive a gift
if your hands
and heart
are closed.

6

Identify with the Unborn
instead of the ego
you fear to lose,
and all will be well.
The Unborn
is constantly emerging.

7

You are born out of the power
and the spirit
and the will
of the Mystery
who longed to be known
and became that
which we are capable of knowing,
God born out of God
into the womb
of our earthly mother,
and from there
into the societal matrix,
where many abide
and never leave.

Yet some
are born out of there
into the awareness
of cosmic realms
where matter and spirit
are recognized
and experienced
as one.
All is God godding.
What joy and peace!

8

What if all the stories,
all the religions,
all the myths,
all the fables,
all science,
all philosophy,
all dance,
all art creations
are simply efforts
by the Hidden
to be Known?
What if it is
an ongoing conversation?
Each flute plays the song
of which it is capable.

9

With true prayer,
you are the glove
that fits God's Hand.
When the glove disappears,
God laughs.
What is this prayer?
What is this praying?
The Joy of Ceaseless Unfolding.

10

Do not look for a God
who is out there,
someone with whom
you must interact.
Instead, experience yourself
and others
as the Cosmos unfolding,
God godding,
the Source sourcing.
No separation.

11

This body is a rope ladder
from Above
on which the Angel of your Being
descends and ascends.
He is all places at once.
His flexible virtuosity
makes you both laugh.

12

Those who held God's tail said,
"God is round and slender."
The trunk-holders scoffed
and said no, "God is round
and fat and long."
Those who held the ear
knew they had the truth:
"God is flat and wide."
The Church of the Tail,
the Church of the Trunk,
and the Church of the Ear
each built separate buildings
and held church suppers.

Each ardently knew
they had the Truth.
The Elephant just laughed.
It shook itself
flinging worshippers
in all directions.
With a smile on its face, it said,
"Those who grasp the truth
know nothing."

13

You will only receive God
according to your capacity.
A teacup
will never contain the ocean.
Smash your cups.
Burst through
all the boundaries
of your heart.

14

Listen
to the singing of the stars
and the roaring of the deep.
The singing opens
to celestial light,
the roaring to unborn depth.
You are in between,
cosmos and chaos
ever forming.

15

When you wake up one day
and realize that your world
is only a fabrication
of your thought system
and only
an infinitesimal possibility
of what is
and what can be—
THEN
you will be truly
awake.

16

When there is only
the Source sourcing,
theistic and atheistic
no longer mean anything.
They are dead categories
from an outmoded worldview.

17

Each of us is accustomed
to think in certain terms.
We generally do not see the world
outside those terms.
We are confined by them.
This is called term-inal illness.

18

Reality
is dealing
with everyone else's
make-believe.
Meanwhile,
do not fall in love
with your own projections.

19

Cannot you see
that you yourself
are the Cross of Suffering?
You stand there
with your arms outspread,
nails on your hands
and on your feet,
and your anxious mind
a crown of thorns.
Cannot you see
that you yourself
are the Crucifixion?

But you are also
the Empty Tomb
of Resurrection!
So laugh
as you walk down the street.
What was inside
is now outside.
Your grave clothes
are folded neatly
and left behind.

20

Disintegration
is essential to transformation.

21

Ancestors
stare through your eyes,
a long procession
reaching back
to Forever.

22

You see
according to
your capacity to see.
When full of yourself,
you do not see much.
Cultivating open space—
capaciousness—
is the key to vision.

23

Being enamored with yourself
is like staring into a flashlight's beam
while walking beneath a full moon.

24

We are like stones
skipping across the sea of eternity.
Every place we touch down
is an incarnation.

25

Your thought system—
what you believe
to be "the truth"—
is only the cage
in which you've shut yourself.
It's the jungle gym of your mind
on which you swing.

26

The physical body
serves as the soul's bookmark
in space-time.
It's the temporary
GPS coordinates
for a soul that's free
to fly
the entire universe.

27

Consciousness
is not something you HAVE.
It's something you ARE.
There is nothing
standing outside
your consciousness
to have it!

28

You don't need
relaxation techniques
or new ways to manage stress.
Instead, you need to learn
to wear the cosmos
like a second skin,
until all idea of skin
evaporates.
And then
you will simply
BE.

29

Of course you are unworthy!
But you're all you've got—
so get over it
and get on with it!

30

Heaven cannot descend
unless you create a landing field.

31

The universe
is far stranger
than you think.
Every time
you try to stuff it
into a belief box
you create a coffin.
And you become the corpse.

32

You cannot see in others
what is not already within you.

33

Lord, forgive me
for being of such little consequence.
Help me to become
even more inconsequential.

34

The caterpillar
thinks the cocoon
it wove around itself
is all there is.
We're not much different.

35

36

The Origin of everything
assumed human form
and walked among us.
Amazing!
And yet,
is this not who we all are
if we but open ourselves
to the truth?

37

The secret of life?
Simply this: Attention!
Your attention
directs energy.
Whatever you attend to
you become.
Instantaneously.

38

Avoid this brand of faulty logic:
"That doesn't exist
because I am incapable
of perceiving it."

39

Have faith
in the rising
and the falling
and the rising again.
Take note,
and you will experience it
day after day:
rising in the morning,
falling in the evening,
and rising again in the morning.
You will see it in the seasons:
rising in the spring,

falling in the winter,
rising again in the spring.
So shall all reality be.
So shall you be.
The signs are set before you;
they are within you
if you would but see.
Again and again,
you will fall and rise,
each time a new forming.
Nothing
is ever lost.

40

This physical body
is a staging area
for the development
of the spiritual body.
Be kind
to your physical body
and each other
while this is going on!

41

Each of us
has our own model
of reality,
based on our capacity
to see.
*Talem eum vidi
qualem capere potui*
(from the Acts of Peter,
in reference to the Transfiguration:
"I saw him in such a form
as I was able to take in").

42

Sit in the seat
at the center of your soul.
Guess Who
is already sitting there?
Whose lap is whose?

43

Why are you so upset
that this "door"
has shut in your face?
To the hinge of a door,
open is the same as shut.

44

When you cling
to any philosophy,
religion,
doctrine,
or worldview,
you are like the ocean
trying to cling
to a floating toothpick
to keep itself
from drowning.

45

Difficulties come
not so much
from not knowing
the right answers,
but from not posing
the right questions.

46

The ego is a wily beast.
You say to yourself,
"my ego,"
as if the ego
were over there somewhere
where you could pick it up,
when all the time,
it's the ego itself
saying, "my ego."

47

If you go down in flames,
shed the most light possible
as you fall.

48

We all tend to belittle
that which we have left behind.
But so long as you belittle it,
you have not actually
left it behind.

49

You come out of Mystery
over which you have no control.
You call this life.
You go into Mystery
over which you have no control.
You call this death.

50

Get one thing straight:
there is no security
in the world.
Security exists only
at the core
of your being.

51

Did you really think
angels dwelt up in the sky?
Don't be silly.
They dwell
in the holy pause
between your inhale
and your exhale.

52

Meditation is pretty simple:
sit down,
shut up,
open up.

53

If you really want
to be somebody,
be the fullest expression
of the nobody
you truly are.

54

Have you noticed
that as you move closer to things
they look bigger?
This is why your problems
overwhelm you.

55

If you think you know
what is going on,
it is a sure sign
that you don't.

56

Aim beyond this lifetime.
Aim for the whole of infinity.
Shoot for the bull's eye
of eternity
Release the arrow
of your life!
Fly with it!

57

Pay attention
to only two things:
one is the eternal Yes
and the other
are the many ways
that Yes is spoken.

58

Don't dare to claim
that you are "spiritual"
when you are actually
dead.
If you are going to live,
you have to move
outside of time.

59

You say you wish
to know the meaning of life,
and yet you keep yourself
occupied
with so many things.
You have placed a sign
on your soul's door:
"Occupied.
Do Not Disturb."
The universe
will respect your request.

60

Some say
there is another world
after this one.
But what if
that world
coexists with *this* world?
What if all
the boundary lines
between "life" and "death"
are only in our minds?
What if life and death
are only mileposts
on an eternal journey
to joyful
consciousness?

61

We come from the divine
and we go to the divine.
In between
we give ourselves hell.

62

Be like our cousins the trees:
be rooted and grounded
while spreading your branches
to the cosmos.

63

Listen carefully!
You will hear your true name—
the name you had
before you let your ego take charge,
when you abandoned love
in exchange for
fear and power.

64

When you fall spiritually asleep,
the Angel of your Being
will pray alone in the wilderness.

65

Each of the world's religions
is a bead on a rosary
worn around God's wrist.

66

Keep climbing out
of every structure ever made.
Let formlessness be your form.
Don't climb into the coffin
of days gone by.
Unless you want to
stretch out on old corpses,
no container can ever
fully
hold you.

67

Get this:
you are your thoughts.
Know this:
if you change your thoughts,
you will change you.
Grasp this:
the more you stare at a thought,
the more powerful it will get.

68

The beliefs
you continue to insist on
create your habit,
a custom-made robe
that tells others
the "holy order"
to which you belong.

69

When you wonder why life
is so difficult,
ask yourself:
What is the purpose
of an obstacle course?

70

When you make the temporal
your temple,
you have short-sheeted
your cosmic bed.

71

When you love
the breath
that breathes you,
You *become*
the breath
that breathes you.
When you become
the breath
that breathes you,
all boundaries fall away.

72

Death is not the cold body
lying on the ground.
Those are only the remains.
Something has escaped.
Be that which escapes
even before
death's escape.
Be your essence.
Die before you die.

73

Theism and atheism
are two peas in a pod,
both dreaming
dreams of triumphant disputes
culminating with
exultant confirmation.
Meanwhile the peapod
and the mother plant
sway in the cosmic wind,
both rooted
in the ground of Being.

74

You cannot solve
the problems produced
by three-dimensional
consciousness
by staying within
three-dimensional
consciousness.
You must become open
to the realm
beyond space-time.

75

Center!
Open!
All else has only
entertainment value.

76

When you rely
on the One-Who-Births-You,
you will arise
like a phoenix
from the ashes of your soul.

77

Ask yourself
only two questions:
Is your heart open
to the plight
of those around you
(human and nonhuman)?
Are you following
the guidance of
the Angel of your Being?

78

All the religions
and philosophies
and socio-political worldviews
are like leaves on a tree.
If all your attention
is stuck to a single leaf,
you'll see neither the whole tree
nor its other leaves.
Take a step back.
Allow the entire tree
to disclose itself,

and you will see now
that all the individual leaves
are integral parts of the whole.
All leaf-bickering ceases.
Each leaf can do its job:
taking in light
and providing nourishment
to the whole tree.

79

The purpose of meditation
is not to accomplish something
but to unaccomplish:
to dismantle the cogno-emotional veil
you use to hide yourself
from the essence of your being.
You are not trying to do something.
You are opening
to the undoing of something.

80

You
are a boundless sea,
and yet you insist
on wearing a life jacket
to keep you from drowning.
How can the sea
drown?

81

If you read the Bible,
don't be looking for words
to comfort and pacify
your little ego—
your sense of yourself
as a small separate self.
Instead seek to amplify
and expand your soul.
Don't look for salve-ation
of the ego:
salving the ego's wounds,
while it remains in its small place,

within its tight boundaries.
Look for new strangeness,
seek boundless realms
previously unimaginable—
and then open yourself.

82

When the veil of the temple
of your heart splits asunder,
when the comfy little illusion
of reality you have woven
is ripped to shreds,
THEN
you will be born.

83

Do you see where Nothing
has yet to come into Being?
Do you see where Everything
has come into Being?
Do you see the space
between the two,
the river that flows
out of Nothingness
into Somethingness?
Meditate from that place.
Live there.
Claim it as your hometown.

This is the place
where your wings
will have room to spread.
Soar.
Be a bird
uncaged.

84

When death
is your companion,
life is rich.
When life
is the only companion
you're willing to have,
you are poor.
Even worse,
you ARE death.

85

As soon as you say
there was a beginning,
you must say
there was something
before the beginning.
As soon as you say
there was something
before the beginning,
you must say
there was nothing
before the something.

As soon as you say
there was nothing
before the something
before the beginning,
you must say
there was nothing
before that nothing.
This is the limit
of ordinary
rational consciousness
(built on ordinal ratios!),
that there is nothing
before the nothing
before the something
before the beginning.

What a mess you get into,
all because you say
there was a beginning!
As soon as you say
here is a this,
you must say
there is a that.
As soon as you say
there is a that,
you have created a gap,
a division.
As soon as you create a division,
you are no longer in relationship.

As soon as you no longer
have a relationship,
you are alienated.
What a mess you get into,
all because you say this
and that and here
and there!
Better
to simply
be
one.

86

The cosmos
did not begin with a Big Bang.
The cosmos is not a male adolescent,
fascinated with the explosive
quick release.
The cosmos began with a Whisper,
an Outbreathing, a Sigh:
the Breath of your Lover in your ear.
The cosmos is still whispering,
still sighing,
still breathing
in your ear.

87

You are the pen
your Source uses
to write on
this Page of Life.

88

Your senses
sense the Source,
and at the same time,
they *are* the Source
sensing.

89

Second-hand living:
Keeping a running commentary
on yourself,
and then thinking that commentary
is yourself.

90

The God you see
is the God you have the capacity
to see.
Shatter the cup,
and water is everywhere.

91

Throw away Occam's razor.
Don't go for the simplest explanation.
Seek the richest one!
The one that opens
treasures of the heart,
the one that fills your heart
with overflowing mystery,
assuming this shape,
now that.
Gods, goddesses,
the Muse, dragons,
alchemical furnaces making gold,
the gold of a strong, sound spirit.

Why settle for simple,
when you can have
all the riches
of Mystery?

92

In *The Wizard of Oz*,
Dorothy's house fell on the witch
and squashed her flat.
Poor Jesus!
His fate wasn't much different.
They built a church
on top of him.

93

What are you doing
looking for a ride
when you are the vehicle?

94

Our attempts to be modest
reveal the egomaniacs we are.
How can you rein in
a nonexistent horse?

95

Do you know what will vanquish
any roots of hell
that burn within you?
Joy,
sheer open-hearted
joy.

96

Where do you hide
your consciousness?
In a flower?
In a book?
In a path of love?
In a look?
Do you hide it in a project?
In your kin?
In your body?
In life's din?
Do you hide it in seek?
Do you seek it in hide?

You could play this game
endlessly.
Time to go
Inside.

97

To know anything,
you must "go native."
You must become
that which you are trying
to understand.
To know God,
you must become God.
Jump—and God will jump into you.
It will be a simultaneous leap
into each other's skin,
laughing and whooping
with the sheer silly joy of it.
Leap into the leaping!

98

How beautiful
that the Source
of all being
would embody as a human!
And that is you, my dear!
That is you!

99

When you take a stance,
the anti-stance
is immediately called into play.
You create your counter-force.
Then you counter
with stronger stance,
which directly strengthens
the opposing force.

100

Light
is the intelligence of the universe.
Love is its heat.
Together, they are the energy
that transforms us,
from self-contained mindsets,
busybodies of the cosmos,
into radiant spheres
of Light and Love.
No mindset needed.

101

You must be careful
how you speak.
When you open your mouth
and thrum your vocal chords,
whole universes
sing themselves into existence.
You must be careful
what you think.
You can damn the world
to hell
in a nanosecond
or bless it with bliss.

102

Your mind contains
vast realms yet unseen.
Howling winds
of arctic windswept plains.
Haunting breezes
from lush equatorial jungles.
You are a mad inventor
sitting inside the labyrinth
of your cavernous mind,
conjuring up some lumination.
Lighting the path
you create as you go
world-shaping.

103

All doctrine is scaffolding
that must drop away
before you can be transformed.
This includes the doctrines of
Who You Think You Are
and
What You Think You Are Not.

104

You
are a sphere of influence
radiating outward in all directions
your moods and your attitudes.
You transform the world around you
through the wavelengths
of the energy you are.
Shitty wavelengths create
a shitty world.
Mediocre wavelengths,
mediocre world.
Joyous wavelengths,
joyous world.

And when two or more spheres
are in radiance together,
a tremendous force
is born.

105

"Without vision,
the people perish,"
is the message from our ancestors.
Your vision,
your imagination,
is both your salvation
and your downfall.
It all depends
on what you envision.

106

Some say,
"When in doubt,
go higher."
My advice to you is this:
When in doubt,
go deeper and wider.

107

We are creatures
who create story.
Story tells us who we are
and what is going on.
Don't belittle another's story.
Bow and bless,
and then fulfill your own.

108

Feelings spring
from the images in your mind.
If you wish to change your feelings,
change your imagery.

109

Give yourself away
to the hungry.
Don't worry.
The soup you are
eternally replenishes.

110

Doubt has a bad reputation.
Don't be a doubting Thomas,
we're told.
I doubt that doubt is bad
Doubt means,
"Well, I don't know about that."
That's a reasonable
and truthful
stance.
Doubt is an antechamber
to knowing.
Just don't be
a professional doubter.

Doubt is *not*
"I don't know about that,
so it's a lie."
A true doubter
searches for knowledge.
Pursue your doubts with vigor
and with an open mind!
Don't make doubt
your religion.

111

Your inner infinity
is as vast as the outer infinity.
Your inner world
is as vast as the outer world.
Go further:
Your inner infinity
and the outer infinity
are one infinity.
Your inner world
and the outer world
are one world.

You are the gateway
between two infinities.
Only when the gate is closed
will you have a problem!

112

Religions
that are alive,
grow.
That doesn't mean
they get fatter,
expanding outward.
It means they grow *up*,
like a tree
or a lotus,
seeking ever more light.
Light-seeking increases
until there are no more bounds,
only light.

When there are no more bounds,
all religions merge.
The cosmos stands
naked and transparent
once again.

113

We are the universe
embodying.
All of us.
Human
and non-human.

114

Do not *make* a living.
BE a living.

115

You are the created
and the uncreated.
The uncreated
is outside space and time,
eternal.
It moves through you,
gives you sustenance,
calls you into being,
promotes your understanding,
deepens your comprehension,
widens your awareness.
The created is the fruit of all this.
The created has a life span.

It will ripen
and drop from the tree.
The uncreated goes on.
Boundless energies flow
from it into you,
bearing wisdom
and light.

116

You are nailed
to the cross
of the spot you are in:
X marks your spot.
The situational weather
around your cross
may change,
but you are always
where you are,
in a fixed position,
unable to move
from your cross
except by dying

And dying is
what will surely happen,
is what you shall surely do.
Die with an open heart.
Nothing more
is asked of you.

117

Do not seek suffering.
Being a human
on earth
is enough.

118

In the temporal world,
you seek to HAVE faith.
In the eternal present,
you ARE faith.

119

Perfect love
is surrender.
Whoever brought you here
will take you home.
Abandon yourself
to your Source
and your Destination.

120

Love requires
the annihilation
of your ego self—
all your stances,
your posturing,
your cajolings,
your whining,
your sarcasms—
all that stuff you treasure,
all that you are convinced
is you.

When you let it all go,
you are finally on the path
to joyful transformation.

121

Four keys to Awareness:
Be aware of attachments.
Detach from attachments.
Detach from detachment.
Laugh.

122

Prayer is not a fish
asking to be rescued
from the river.
Prayer is learning
to swim in the river.

123

You have access to
personal energy
and universal energy.
The first is limited,
the latter limitless.
Your thoughts arise
from both realms.
Thought arising
out of personal energy
is generally chatter
about self
and its beloved trio:
I, me, and mine.

It rattles on forever,
unable to bear silence.
Meanwhile, silence is the well
from which universal energy flows.
Personal energy
is temporal, linear,
based on causes and effects.
Universal energy
is constantly unfolding
in the Eternal Now.

124

When you live
in the world of time and space,
you frantically seek security,
where no security
will ever be found.
When you live
in the Eternal Now,
you live in the relaxed security
of no security at all.

125

There are two modes of being.
The first worries
about "wasting time."
It uses life
to accomplish things,
to "get things done."
The second
loves life as it unfolds,
allowing creativity to flow
from life's infinite wellsprings.

126

Grace.
Mercy.
Holy companionship.
Allow these three arrows
from the Divine quiver
to pierce
your heart.

127

When you are born again,
you are born out of the temporal,
into the Eternal Now.

128

Since you do not know
what you do not know,
why are you so certain
about your boundaries?

129

When you stand
apart from others,
viewing yourself as separate,
you will do one of two things:
Feel a need
for a "plan of salvation,"
a means of reconciliation
to bring you back into the fold.
Or stand
"bloody but unbowed"
and shake your fist
at the world.

Unity with the cosmos
requires
a far different outlook.

130

What would your life
be like if you knew,
deeply and thoroughly,
that you are the cosmos
embodying,
that you are the cosmos
at play?

131

Your mindset is not reality,
nor is it a scientific fact,
nor sacred ground.
It is no better
and no truer
than any of the other mindsets
walking around you.
A mindset is merely
a collection
of mental habits.

132

You embody
heaven and earth.
You are a ladder
planted on the ground
that reaches into the sky.
Angel energy ascends
and descends
the ladder of your life,
bringing heaven to earth
and earth to heaven.

133

You
are a key
on the cosmic piano.
Each person,
each animal,
each plant,
each "thing,"
has its own key.
Together,
each with its own note,
the keys play the same Song.
Can you hear it?

134

You cannot see
the soul I am
unless you see
with the eyes
of the soul you are.
I cannot see
the soul you are
unless I see you
with soul eyes.
We cannot see
with soul eyes
unless we move beyond appearance,
unless we see *through* appearance.

When your eyes stop
at the surface
of others and of the world,
you live in a superficial world.
Go deeper
and you will transform
yourself
and the world around you.
"Deep calls unto deep."

135

What does it mean
to be "born again"?
It means to be birthed
out of the realm of appearance,
born not of water
(the amniotic fluid of your first birth)
but of spirit
(The-One-Who-Breathes-Us).
Now you are a spiritual being.
You see and move
through time
and outside time,
for Love knows no time.

136

When your mind is filled
with the usual stuff,
you will not see
beyond the usual stuff.
Miracles and wonders surround you,
but you will see only
your fear,
your anger,
your worry.
Do you want to see more?
Create room in your mind.
Have a garage sale
and get rid of all that stuff.

Better yet,
put it out by the curb
for the garbage man.

137

You get up in the morning
and put on the same old clothes,
dressing yourself
in the thought patterns
of yesterday
and yesteryear
and yester-decade.
Today,
why not go naked?

138

Don't look
for a new plan of salvation!
Find solace only
in the burning flame of your heart.
This is where new birth arises!
Experience God in a new way.
Learn the steps of his Eternal Tango,
the Tango of the Blazing Heart.

139

Shed your doctrinal clothes.
Step naked
into the roaring flames
of the alchemical furnace.
Be transformed in the fire.
One will walk with you there,
the same One
who walked with Daniel
in his fiery furnace.
You will never know this One,
for to "know" is to possess.

No one can possess
the Eternal One
who is with you
in your flaming heart.

140

When you live only
in the World of Appearance,
you know only
the world's outer skin
and know nothing
of what lies beneath.
Even when Mystery
pokes through the world's skin,
you do not see It.
You believe the world
holds nothing that is hidden.

Instead, be one who lives
in the World of Appearance
while your feet walk another Ground.
Then you will know
that nothing is hidden
for it is all right there
when you have eyes to see.

141

All mystics,
no matter their religion,
have removed
the doctrinal clothing
from their hearts,
and stepped naked
into the same Heart.
When they meet,
they laugh
and dance together
the same Heart Dance.

Meanwhile,
when theologians
from separate religions meet,
they may try to convince
the others
of the error of their ways.
Mystics have a party.
Theologians a debate.

142

Whatever we follow,
we become.
When we follow music,
we become music.
When we follow justice,
we become justice.
When we follow understanding,
we become understanding.
Whatever we follow, we become.
If you follow the God-Man Jesus.
you embody
the Unseen and the Seen.
You follow Heart-Music and Joy.

Whatever you follow,
you become.
When you follow the God-Man,
you will become a god-man.
The tree will bear fruit.

143

What is the key
to joyful awareness?
Laughter.
Genuine hearty (from the heart)
laughter
produces space in your mind.
It gives you greater capacity
for awareness.
But it only comes
when you surrender
to whatever *is*
and stop taking yourself
so seriously.

144

Each of us has a personal god.
You may not call your god
God,
but there is something in your life
you worship above all else.
The greater the radiance
of your god,
the greater your radiance.
The more smudgy your god,
the more smudgy you are.
The light you shed reveals your god.
You become the god
you serve.

145

Your ego is the way
you have learned to maneuver
through the external world.
Your ego is a collection
of learned habits
for manipulating the material world.
No matter how effective they may be
in the world you see and touch,
they're useless in the spiritual world.
A different vehicle is needed there,
one that has nothing to do
with the ego.

146

The spiritual world
requires habits opposite
from those you've learned
for maneuvering your ego
through the material world.
The ego blames, judges,
clings, desires, and suspects.
It is greedy,
self-admiring,
self-doubting,
contemptuous,
scared, noisy,
and half asleep.

The Self who learns to maneuver
through the spiritual world
is open, loving,
calm, and quiet.
It is accepting,
giving and forgiving,
surrendering,
and energizing.
It is diamond sharp,
relentless,
joyfully aware,
and knows no bounds.

147

Your ego
is the scab
that's formed over the wound
in your heart.
Open your wound
to the Wellspring of healing,
the Source that birthed
and breathes you.
Become a radiant sphere.

148

You move through your day
riding the waves of emotion
and societal demands.
Even if you take a few moments
in your prayer closet
or on your meditation mat,
when you're done,
you slam the door behind you
and leap on a wave,
when all the while
another sea waits
within you,
a sea of Energetic Mercy.

149

Worry
is the repeated visualization
of disaster.
It is a demonic prayer form.
Whatever you visualize,
you are.
When you visualize disaster,
you experience that disaster.
Physiologically,
every cell of your body responds
as if that disaster
is actually taking place.
Therefore it is.

To worry is to forecast doom,
and to lend energy
to making that doom happen.
A worrier is a conjurer
of black magic.
The antidote to worry
is not positive thinking,
floating around pretending
everything is butterflies and roses.
The antidote
is to go out of your mind.
Leave the worry behind
and dance
in the
Eternal
Now.

150

You build explanations
for the world's Mystery,
islands of convenience
upon which you erect
rigid structures
to describe the Ocean
that surrounds you.
You stay there
on your little island,
believing the structures you built
are holy temples,

gazing in puzzlement
and condemnation
at other islands
and their structures.
When you see
the Tsunami of the Spirit
coming your way,
be glad.
Prepare to leave your island
and become
the Ocean.

151

Listen!
A gentle
and powerful
Spirit is calling you,
wooing you,
reminding you
of that from which you came.
The Spirit asks you to return
to the Spirit of yourself,
to the small light that still burns
like an ember
in the ashes of your being.

152

Don't look over your shoulder,
back at what used to be.
This wound in your heart
is a portal
to something new.

153

To live in the Spirit
is to follow the Radiant Beam.
Straight is its Way,
and narrow is its Path.
Yet it is closer
than your very breath.
Be careful.
When you say you "have" this Light,
you don't.
You will never have It.
But this Radiant Beam
of Grace and Light and Knowing
has you.

154

Water gives itself freely.
It will rest as easily within a cup
as in no cup at all.
If a cup says it is the *only* cup,
it forgets that its only purpose
is to hold water.
Cups proclaim their cuppiness,
and cup-worship forms.
Cup wars break out.
Meanwhile, water has its way
and flows as it will.

Does this meditation
make you condemn
the cups you know?
Be careful!
This condemnation
is only more cuppiness.
Be water.

155

Stop being so pleased with yourself.
Stop being so hard on yourself
Have no thoughts of yourself at all.
When these thoughts arise,
smile at them gently,
and let them go.

156

You can't help but interpret
the meaning of your life.
Remember, though:
any interpretation you create
is a shroud.
You'll want to band together
with those wearing similar
shrouds,
and separate yourself
from those whose shrouds
are different from yours.
Cast the shroud off your soul.
Shrouds are for the dead,
not the living.

157

There are two forms of awareness:
One imposes itself upon the world
and tries to wrestle the world
into submission.
The other allows the world
to simply
disclose itself.
Which do you think is more joyful?

158

You burn
for that which you do not have,
creating a small version of hell,
your own personal hell.
Instead, be fire,
and then no fire can burn you.
All that you desire
is already inside you.
You are a child of Mystery,
offsping of the Source.
When you truly know that,
you will leave your hell.
The heat
will change
to light.

159

Let your wound
become a mouth
that speaks your truth.

160

When you understand
there is no past, no future,
you will live in Now,
free
from all that space-and-time baggage
you've been carrying around.
You will float
in the Eternal Flow
that is forever
coming into Being.

161

If you insist on having a self,
you will believe in this illusion,
and you, like Adam and Eve, will
Fall.
Separated from the interflow,
you will cast yourself
out of the Garden.
But each moment
you have a choice.
You are free to come back
Home.

162

Your body is the cocoon
in which the Life-Force Spirit
does its work
to transform your Soul.
Yield yourself
to this transformation
so that when the time comes
to leave the cocoon,
you are ready
to spread your wings.

163

Transform
into that which you already are.
Reclaim your birthright.

164

You are an arrow
aimed at a target.
Release the arrow.
Let it fly.
You will end up
in the center
of your own heart.

165

Deny yourself.
Take up your cross daily.
This means to deny
your favorite images of yourself.
Whatever it is—
misunderstood tragic hero,
victim, fixer, holy icon—
don't fall for the glamour.
Deny it.
Stand fully present
in the present.
Accept whatever comes.
This is your cross.

This is your labor.
And this is how
you will know
and express
love.

166

You ask,
"If all is interflowing,
why do I feel so separate?"
The answer is this:
Your need to be in control
is what separates you from the Flow.
Relax your need for control.
Let it go,
and all separation
will disappear.

167

To understand something,
you must be willing to become it.
Mere observation will not do.

168

Celebrate,
for a child is born.
Who is this child?
You.
You are being born
again and again.
Newness unfurls in you,
like a flame rising
from a burning log.
The log is turning to ash,
even as the flame
leaps ever higher
into the air.

When you realize this,
you will laugh out loud
in surprised joy.

169

Stop
just plowing along
on the horizontal plane.
Open yourself to the vertical.
Lift up your spiritual head.
Aspire to the Above!

170

You are a gate
between two worlds.
You are a gateway to the Divine.
Now become unhinged.

171

You are nailed
to the cross of time and space.
But at the same time,
you are eternally resurrecting,
forever transforming.
The you that you are today
is not the you of yesterday,
nor even the you
of a few seconds ago.
Crucifixed and resurrecting,
that's the crux of the matter
that has no matter
at all.

172

Look at Jesus
as an icon rather than an idol.
An icon is to be seen THROUGH,
not gazed AT.
An icon is a window,
opening to the boundless sublime.
Leap through that opening
into pure joy,
a joy that is all inclusive,
leaving no one
and nothing
behind.

173

The Mystery
that calls you into being
is loving, jovial,
adventurous, and daring.
He is friendly,
forgiving,
takes no prisoners,
and He is always waiting
for you to laugh with Him,
get off your butt,
and join the dance.

174

If you want to think of yourself
as a Christian,
don't think that means
you follow Christ.
It means to BE Christ.
All bread you eat
is your own flesh.
All wine you drink
is your own blood.
You are a child of the Father,
and you know it.
You are an offspring
of the Wellspring
that is forever springing.

175

Forget about sin.
Instead,
worry about losing your Soul.
The law is dead
without the Spirit.
Morals do not immerse you
in the current ever flowing
from the One,
without whom you do not exist.

176

We understand
only through metaphors.
So we say we are
"children of the Living God,"
because that metaphor
warms our hearts
more than to say we are
"fractals of the Fractal Interflow."
Yet both say the same.

177

Once you go through a door,
you don't need to go through it
again and again.
No matter how sacred or holy
the door appears,
you move through
to the other side,
to the next room.

178

The Immovable Mind
of martial arts
means that your attention
is not caught by anything.
Your mind is not stuck
in a memory.
Your mind is not caught
in a fantasy.
Your mind is not snagged
by fear or anger
or any other emotion.

You mind does not stand
staring at your reflection,
worrying about how you're doing
or what others think of you.
Instead, the mind is like water
reflecting the moon.
It does not contain the moon,
it only mirrors it.
And then
Immovable Mind
allows you to move
because you are
no longer
stuck, caught, or snagged
by the tar baby
of your ego.

179

Meditation
is not a hypnotic state.
Meditation is wide-awake
awareness.

180

May your mind
have wings.
May you be
continuously inspired.
May you use the keys
to joyful awareness
that have always been yours,
for they are your
birthright.

About the Author

There are astronauts and cosmonauts, those who sail the skies and the cosmos, who voyage into the external universe—but George Breed considers himself to be an intranaut, a voyager into the mystery of the inner realms. He is a warrior, a mystic, a healer, and a wise guy.

A fifth-degree black belt as well as a prolific writer, George has shared his wisdom in several books, including the following titles published by Anamchara Books: *The Hidden Words of the Living Jesus: A Commentary on the Gospel of Thomas* and *Jesus & Lao Tsu: Adventures with the Tao Te Ching*, and two books coming in 2015, *The Inner Work of the Warrior* and *Zen Baptist*. George deliberately has no car and walks daily in the beauty of northern Arizona, almost always with a camera. He is a man who has traveled far on his journey of transformation and consciousness. You can find out more about him on his Facebook page.

The Hidden Words
of the Living Jesus
Author: George Breed

In 1934, Egyptian farmers dug up a clay jar filled with ancient Coptic manuscripts. Among them was the Gospel of Thomas, a collection of Jesus' sayings, some familiar to us, some new, all with a fresh slant to their implications. In *The Hidden Words of the Living Jesus*, George Breed casts the light of his spiritual wit over these mysterious sayings. As simply conversational as it is deeply provocative, his commentary invites us to journey more deeply into the spiritual realm, accompanied always by the living Jesus.

Jesus and Lao Tzu:
Adventures with
the Tao Te Ching
Author: George Breed

"How can I describe this book? If I say it is brilliant, crazy, hilarious, sobering, vulgar, and sublime, all those words are true—but they are certainly not enough to express the contents of *Jesus & Lao Tzu*. The book defies being categorized or neatly summarized. It will have to suffice if I say simply this: the book's words make me happier, freer, and wiser. If you read it with an open heart, I predict it will do the same for you."
—*Kenneth McIntosh, author of* Water from an Ancient Well: Celtic Spirituality for Modern Life

Books to inspire your spiritual journey.

In Celtic Christianity, an *anamchara* is a soul friend, a companion and mentor (often across the miles and the years) on the spiritual journey. Soul friendship entails a commitment to both accept and challenge, to reach across all divisions in a search for the wisdom and truth at the heart of our lives.

At Anamchara Books, we are committed to creating a community of soul friends by publishing books that lead us into deeper relationships with God, the Earth, and each other. These books connect us with the great mystics of the past, as well as with more modern spiritual thinkers. They are designed to build bridges, shaping an inclusive spirituality where we all can grow.

To find out more about Anamchara Books and order our books, visit **www.AnamcharaBooks.com** today.

Vestal, New York 13850
www.AnamcharaBooks.com

www.ingramcontent.com/pod-product-compliance
Lightning Source LLC
Chambersburg PA
CBHW060521080526
44586CB00012B/562